# REVOLUTION WITHOUT VIOLENCE

Dedicated to my wife Maggie, my true and enduring soulmate.

# REVOLUTION WITHOUT VIOLENCE

## AN ORDINARY MAN'S GUIDE TO PEACE AND PROSPERITY IN A DANGEROUS WORLD

---

**Rob Noyes-Smith**

Cover artwork created by F. Zia.

*Revolution Without Violence: An Ordinary Man's Guide to Peace and Prosperity in a Dangerous World*
Written by: Rob Noyes-Smith

Library of Congress Control Number: 2012939674

ISBN: 978-1-938158-02-5

Copyright © 2012
Emergent Publications,
3810 N. 188th Ave, Litchfield Park, AZ 85340, USA

All rights reserved. No part of this publication may be reproduced, stored on a retrieval system, or transmitted, in any form or by any means, electronic, mechanical, photocopying, microfilming, recording or otherwise, without written permission from the publisher.

Printed in the United States of America

## ACKNOWLEDGEMENTS

First, I must thank my family for their support, in particular Dave, who invited me into very personal and private occasions.

Second my "Ante" group: Jan Maples, Kevin Reid, Tony DellaFlora and Karen King. This group has been meeting monthly for 17 years, the name comes from our purpose, to up the Ante. This group is as diverse politically as the country but, we are there for each other, through thick and thin, committed to exploring our personal depths and holding each other accountable.

Third, all the wonderful people who have read drafts and given me their feedback. Of particular note, Tony DellaFlora of Taos Communications Empire, and Ron Schultz of Emergent Publications, who assiduously worked through many expanded versions editing and cutting with love.

Lastly, Tom Brokaw, who graciously replied to one of my earlier versions with a note of encouragement.

*Rob Noyes-Smith*

## ABOUT THE AUTHOR

**Rob Noyes-Smith** has lived and worked in eight different countries on four continents. His careers span from army officer, owning five businesses to executive coach. He lives with his wife Maggie in Albuquerque New Mexico. They have three sons.

# CONTENTS

## PROLOGUE .................................. 9
The Funeral ...................................................................9

Fathers and Sons ..........................................................16

Introduction .................................................................18

## CHAPTER 1
## FINDING ANSWERS FROM WITHIN .. 23
Meditate in Malawi or Sit and Fish on the
Banks of the Zambezi ...................................................29

## CHAPTER 2
## THE PAST .................................. 41
The Three Fs .................................................................45

## CHAPTER 3
## SCENARIO PLANNING ....................... 53
Possible Nuclear War Scenario One ..............................56

Possible Nuclear War Scenario Two ..............................57

Possible Nuclear War Scenario Three ...........................59

Possible War Scenario Four ..........................................59

Possible War Scenario Five ...........................................60

Possible War Scenario Six .............................................60

Possible War Scenario Seven ........................................62

Possible War scenario Eight .........................................63

## CHAPTER 4
## THE POLITICAL ........................ 67

## CHAPTER 5
## THE PEOPLE ........................... 71
The Process ..................................................... 72
Some Years Later after the funeral ............................. 75

## EPILOGUE
## FINANCIAL MELTDOWN ..................... 79
A New Day in Politics .......................................... 84
Weight Reduction Ideas ......................................... 92
Exercises to Strengthen the Heart (the Economy),
the Muscle of Production. ...................................... 97

## APPENDIX A
## FURTHER POSSIBLE
## OUT-OF-THE-BOX IDEAS FOR
## HELPING THE ECONOMY .................. 103

## APPENDIX B
## FURTHER IDEAS FOR
## CONSIDERATION REGARDING
## POLITICIANS ......................... 109
Wrap Up ......................................................... 111

*Any intelligent fool can make things bigger, more complex, and more violent. It takes a touch of genius—and a lot of courage—to move in the opposite direction.*

> Attributed to Albert Einstein.

# PROLOGUE

This book emerged as the result of attending a funeral with my son. The emotions that flooded in around the loss of such a precious life and all those that had gone before caused an ache that had to be resolved. Therefore, I introduce the book with the funeral in order to set the context, in order to ask, are we doomed to repeat our history of war after war after war? Do we have the capacity as humans to change our future from more death and destruction to a more peaceful, happier world?

### The Funeral

On June 28, 2005, a four-man Navy SEALs reconnaissance unit, high in the Afghanistan mountains bordering Pakistan, was attacked by a large force of Taliban insurgents. The unit called in the rapid deployment group—eight SEALs and an eight-man Night Stalker crew—aboard a large, twin-blade helicopter. While the ship was trying to land at 10,000 feet in the rugged mountain terrain, the insurgents fired a rocket-propelled grenade, striking the helicopter and killing everyone inside.

The original four remaining SEALs on the ground fought a running battle. Three died: Matt Axelson, Danny Dietz and Michael Murphy. The fourth, Marcus Luttrell, though wounded, managed to evade his attackers and escape. Eventually, with the help of a local sheepherder, he found his way to safety.[1]

The battle resulted in the biggest single-day loss of life in the history of the Navy SEALs, that is, until August 8th 2011 when twenty two SEALs were among the 30 American forces, seven Afghan commandoes and one interpreter, killed when their helicopter was shot down in Afghanistan.

My son Dave is a Navy SEAL.

It was early July, a Wednesday night, when I spoke to Dave by phone. He had just attended his third funeral in five days. He told me, his voice trembling, how moving this last one had been. It seemed as though the whole of Long Island had closed down.

The route was lined with police, and at regular intervals local fire departments had parked their fire engines with their ladders extended above the road, forming an arch. Crowds of silent people lined the route at every turn.

Dave said it was a life-changing experience. This wasn't the time, on the telephone, to explore what he meant by that, so I asked him if I could visit him soon. He told me that the next day he had to drive to Dover, Delaware, to escort the body of Matt Axelson, the last SEAL recovered from the battle, back to his hometown of Chico, California.

---

1. See the book "Lone Survivor" by Marcus Luttrell.

Dave arrived in California with the casket on Friday, and was again struck by the courtesy and respect afforded him and the deceased by the airlines and the public. Matt's family held a memorial service in Cupertino on Sunday, and the funeral was to be held in his hometown of Chico on the following Thursday.

I flew to Sacramento on Tuesday evening, and after Dave and I booked into the hotel, we found a quiet Italian restaurant downtown and relaxed over a beer. It was rare to find ourselves just one-on-one with no distractions. Our mood was light but there was the undercurrent sense of why we were here together.

I let Dave talk, with just the occasional question for clarification. It had been a tough ten days for him. The first funeral had been in Boulder City, Nevada. Being there to comfort the parents, seeing to many of the military details necessary to coordinate such an event, and meeting SEALs flying in from different places at different times took a lot of arranging. Then he was off to Hawaii, New York, and now, California to repeat the process.

Most people do their best to understand this kind of situation, but unless you've been there, committed to your buddies *beyond anything else, above anything else,* you can't really know. We shared a common background. I had been in Special Forces myself, and thus this shared knowledge that needed no explanation existed. This was not father-son intimacy; this was Special Forces intimacy.

"What was life-changing?" I eventually asked Dave.

"Normally you don't think of the military as getting much respect," he said. "But this support, this genuine outpouring, not just in the streets but at the reception afterwards, was so stunning, so moving. Well, I feel a renewed commitment to the cause, as a way to honor my fallen friends."

"Any revenge motives?" I gently probed.

"Any thinking person knows it has nothing to do with revenge. It's about doing the job."

For me, hearing my son's words was a double-edged sword. On the one hand, I felt very proud of him and on the other I felt very parental: that tightening of the throat and around the heart, that fear that every parent has for the safety of his or her children. I had almost hoped that he felt the opposite, that he now opposed the war, thought it was a bloody waste and didn't agree with how it is being conducted.

I decided to postpone any internal debate and just be with Dave, just live in his world for the three days we had together. Be sad, be happy, be open to it all.

The next day we drove the two hours to Chico, stopping for lunch on the way. It was marvelous listening to his ideas, being on his timetable, not mine, suddenly being the junior partner, not the dad who had all the answers. It was a passage of life, the realization that I'd raised a child who was now fully independent, with whom I could relate, man-to-man, not father-to-son, and that I'd done a good job.

We got to the hotel mid-afternoon, and by this time, Dave's phone was ringing constantly with calls from other SEALs checking in from around the country regarding the arrangements.

The next morning we were up early for breakfast, and the dining room was filling with SEALs of every rank, all of them in dress blues. After breakfast we left in convoy to the funeral site where the SEALs rehearsed for the ceremony. Fortunately, the day was cloudy and not going to be the usual 100 degrees, making the outdoor ceremony a lot more tolerable.

People started to arrive, old and young, relatives and friends, and many couples with small children and babies. It was the first Navy funeral I had ever attended and the familiar pride in our country, in our men and women, surged through my chest. I held it together until the folding and presentation of the flag. Then the tears flowed uncontrollably. At the end of the ceremony, everyone filed up one by one to pay their last respects. I again felt the flood of emotion over the loss of such a wonderful man's life and the loss of so much potential. But for a few weeks—Dave's deployment had finished just three weeks before the battle—this could have been my own son.

Everyone drove slowly to a country club for the reception. Matt's best friend from high school and college struggled through his speech, followed by others, including the SEAL admiral. Afterward, lunch was served and people mingled. Dave introduced me to Matt's parents, Donna and Corky, and to Cindy, his wife, and her parents. I had thought to not impose and just stay in the background, but because of Dave's speech at the memorial service for Matt on the previous Sunday, his family had expressed a wish to meet me.

At that previous Sunday's memorial service, Donna had asked Dave, somewhat belatedly, to say something about Matt. With only a couple of minutes to prepare, he decided to tell a funny story about when Matt had just joined the team and Dave decided to mess with the rookie on a training swim around Ford Island.

The story took the somber assembly by surprise and sent them into gales of laughter, which many now say was what they needed. Thus came the request for an introduction when they learned that I was coming to the funeral. It wasn't me they needed to meet, but they needed someone, some place, to repose their gratitude for Dave, because he had helped them feel so much better.

I can only assume that this outpouring of gratitude for Dave was a way of honoring Matt and his chosen profession, a physical outlet for their thoughts and feelings and a way to begin the process of closure, which is the purpose of a funeral. For me, it was easy to bask in such kudos. No doubt our similar looks made it easy for anyone to discern we were father and son, and after a while I stopped being surprised at people approaching me to tell me how wonderful he was. I heard this from many of the SEALs who had flown in for the occasion, telling me of Dave's professionalism and leadership, and it added to the glow I felt.

Gradually the crowd started to thin out. I was standing at the buffet table with a half-prepared plate, talking to a guest. As he moved on and I resumed my selection, I realized that I may have been holding up someone on my right.

"Excuse me, would you like to go ahead?" I asked a woman I had not met before.

"No," she said. "I would like to talk to you about your son and what a marvelous job he did at the memorial service. We, as a family, would like to adopt him and put him in our prayers. Could you send me a photo of him so the children know what he looks like?"

During this request, I had been looking into her eyes. I didn't know who she was, but perhaps because we were both so emotionally vulnerable, we allowed the look to go deep, to our very souls.

Not breaking eye contact, I quietly asked her, "Where do you get such peace and tranquility so deep inside?"

She replied, "The Lord."

And I knew it to be true.

She was Matt's aunt, married to a pastor, with three children, two teenagers and a ten-year-old. Neither her husband nor the children were at the funeral, which is why she wanted the photo of Dave, so that she could show it to her family. At that point Dave joined us and I explained the request. He seemed genuinely pleased.

It was time to leave. Emotionally drained, we went back to the hotel for an afternoon nap. I tossed and turned, unable to sleep. I realized that it was probably because of me that all three of my sons had joined the military.

**Fathers and Sons**

I was born in Coventry, England. For the first three years of my life, I didn't see my father. He was away, fighting in World War II in North Africa. When he finally came home, my mother told me, I didn't stop holding his hand for three days. All I'd had was a picture of him in uniform, prominently displayed in our two-room flat, and my mother's explanation of why he wasn't there. He was away doing important business, fighting the bad guys. This was necessary, of course, in case he didn't make it home, a possibility that nearly came true on several occasions. When my father did return, he rarely spoke of the war. I, along with my schoolboy friends in similar circumstances, embellished what little we knew.

I remember him taking me to see a war film. I must have been six years old, and it involved a battle fought against the Germans over a particular farmhouse. After the movie, he told me that was what he had to do. Of course he was my hero. Not only had he come home, but he had won the war.

At around ten years old, I began reading books that had come out describing different men's adventures fighting in World War II. *Reach for the Sky* was one, the story of Douglas Bader, who had lost his legs in a plane crash before the war, but who convinced the Royal Air Force to let him fly Spitfires again until he was shot down and ended up in a German prisoner-of-war camp. *The Great Escape, The Colditz Story, The Battle of the River Plate,* and the many stories of the Battle of Britain followed. All I wanted to be was a Spitfire pilot.

All these stories fed a young boy's desire to be adventurous, tough, and of course, a hero. My father was still in the Territorial Army (the reserves), and my mother was secretary to the major who ran the unit. I remember listening to the stories that Major Brooks told of his service in Kenya, living in tents in hot, dry, desert conditions. It was all so romantic, and I willingly put that picture in my brain as an adventure I wanted to experience.

And where did I end up? By age eighteen I was in the Federation of Rhodesia and Nyasaland (now three independent countries, Zimbabwe, Zambia and Malawi) doing precisely that as an officer in the King's African Rifles.

So there are two points here: first, the need for adventure and to prove myself to other men as being courageous and tough. Second, that what you plant in your subconscious will take you kicking and screaming toward it.

Regarding our sons, I'm sure that as they were growing up in Canada and the United States, the stories of Africa that my wife Maggie and I told of close encounters with elephant, lion, and hippo caught their own imaginations. This was no doubt supplemented when two of my dearest friends, old Special Forces mates, came to live near us in Toronto and related their experiences. These stories, just like those Major Brooks told me, probably stuck in my sons' subconscious minds and subsequently influenced them to join up. Do we, therefore, fathers and sons, help perpetuate war through our own personal history, or is it much deeper than that?

The evening after the funeral, Dave and I were invited by Cindy, Matt's wife, to join her and friends for drinks in Matt's favorite Irish pub in Chico. There were about 35 people, between the ages of 25 and 35, some single, some the parents of the little babies I had noticed at the funeral. Of course, we were not allowed to buy a drink, and with many rounds and toasts to Matt, the party got loose and raucous quickly. There were moments when I viewed the scene uninterrupted from a quiet corner. I observed the energy, that irrepressibleness of young people in charge of their own lives, searching and striving to make their mark. Their sense of being immortal, impregnable, undaunted, which had just been momentarily shattered, was eagerly clawing its way back through booze and laughter. I could remember having done the same thing myself, many times.

### Introduction

I left the funeral and my time with Dave to return to my own world. I have had a number of different careers, from army officer, stockbroker, and insurance broker to working for an American company in Hong Kong. These experiences, along with owning four different businesses in energy, food, printing, and consulting in three different countries, have brought me to my current occupation of management consulting and executive coaching with clients in different parts of the United States while living in Albuquerque, New Mexico, with my wife Maggie, the three boys all grown and gone.

It became obvious to me, as an ordinary citizen with no affiliation with some think tank or the ideologies of the right or the left, that while we look for some elected person or candidate to solve our problems, there is no one person who knows all the answers or who can even deliver on their promises.

Despite many good intentions by many candidates, the current political swamp called Washington will suck any elected leader into the thickly entangled web of intrigue, influence and money. The primary legitimate power for the ordinary citizen is the ballot box, yet we are constantly disappointed with the lack of results. All the while, the news from around the world becomes worse. Horrible killings and bombings that seem out of our control threaten our very existence.

This situation led me to the fundamental question: *How do we, the people, without resorting to violence, exert power so that those in power (the government and the shadowy money influencers who control the politicians), cannot ignore us, dismiss us, or crush us?*

If there is no one out there, no knight on a white horse, then I must rely upon myself and find the answers within myself. Over the years, when in difficult situations, I have been aware of a wise inner voice that has come to my aid. Why can I not call on this voice now? Surely all I need to do is ask and be prepared to listen.

Once I started to write, the conversation between my day-to-day conscious ego mind and the previously secluded, subconscious part of me blossomed into a very fruitful animated dialogue. It seems that this previously untapped part of me has been patiently waiting for the opportunity to come forth and be listened to. It seems that this is where all my past experiences accumulate with their lessons and wisdom. Further, it seems that through my prayers and meditation, this is the pathway for tapping into the metaphysical, the spiritual, my higher self. But I am also highly circumspect in this regard. There are too many people who claim to talk to God and thus claim to be justified in committing heinous crimes. All discussions and solutions must therefore ultimately bear the mantle of personal responsibility, not of some decree that eludes accountability.

In order to distinguish the two parts of the conversation, I have named the day-to-day part of me E for ego and the wise part of me WO for Wise One.

## CHAPTER 1

# FINDING ANSWERS FROM WITHIN

E: So what do you think about those young people we met at the pub after the funeral?

WO: They labor in the valley of proof.

E: What do you mean?

WO: Let's talk about the journey of life and the role that ego plays in your development. The valley of proof is the period of life when the ego is trying to establish its own separate identity, but let's go back to your early years.

When you were very young, probably just eighteen months old, you were walking from your grandma's house by yourself up the street toward the main thoroughfare, Coundon Road. In front of you were the big billboards attached to the Coventry Rugby Grounds' fence. Suddenly your reality changed, you had a vision where the billboards had been. Your vision was of the Planet Earth and you saw millions of little black dots, like ants, moving from continent to continent.

Because you were so young and had not fully developed your left-brain reasoning powers, you were open to seeing different realities. This was somewhat the same as the astronauts seeing Planet Earth for the first time from space and realizing we are all one. You got exactly the same impression, we are all one.

Do you remember?

E: Of course. I periodically forget it in the hubbub of life, but I remember it clearly.

WO: This was when you and I were one, before the incident in your grandma's backyard when you got locked out of the house. Do you remember that time?

E: I was roughly two years old. My mom and I had gone to see my grandma which probably meant it was a Sunday because it was still wartime and Mom had to work six days a week. I had walked out into the back yard and pulled the back door shut. I played in the air-raid shelter for a while then tried to go back inside the house. Somehow the back door had locked, and try as I might, I couldn't budge it. I then tried calling out and banged on the door with my tiny fists, but got no response. I listened intently and could just hear their voices emanating from the front room. I redoubled my efforts at knocking and shouting but, again, no one heard me. I started to cry, feeling bereft and alone. Surely they must hear me, surely they won't abandon me.

After some time I came to the realization that if I was to get out of there, I would have to do it myself. I wiped my tears and set about exploring the six-foot garden gate to the alley alongside the house. It too was locked and I couldn't move it. Perhaps the neighbor's gate to the same alley would open. I somehow squeezed through the common garden fence that got me into next door's yard. I ran to their alley gate, and, miraculously, it opened. I ran down the alley and around to the front door where I banged again. This time they heard me and came to the door, totally surprised to see me. Immediately I began a sobbing story of my escape, which brought hugs and pacification. But the die had been cast; I had made the decision to stand on my own two feet, take care of myself, and make things happen.

WO: Yes, this was your point of departure from me, your wise inner self. Every person has just such a point, although most don't remember it so clearly, the point at which you set out on your journey to become your individual self, the loss of innocence, you might say. Your reality at this point is that there is only you, and this is called ego. From here on until some later point in life, you and ego are as one, and hence you live in what I call the valley of proof. The valley of proof is just that, a valley where your view of life is limited and hence your perspective is limited. For a good portion of the world's population, this perspective is limited to physical survival, obtaining the next meal. Those of you who are lucky enough to progress beyond physical survival continue to encounter ego survival. The ego is always fearful that the roof will fall in and therefore it is constantly trying to control the circumstances, the environment, and, often, other people in order to feel safe. Everyone goes through this process of proving to the world, and ultimately to yourself, that you are worthy, worthy of being accepted by others, worthy of being loved by others, worthy of loving yourself, and, should you believe in Universal Intelligence (I use this description of God because I know that the word God always conjures up a childhood image for you of a huge man in the sky with a long white beard who sends bolts of lightening to strike the sinful, a relic of your early exposure to the church), then worthy of being loved by Universal Intelligence. It is a reality created by humans, a separation reality, that is an illusion, for I and Universal Intelligence are never separate from you; we are always there, always ready to be co-joined, to be one.

E: Is there a definite age or time when this co- joining, this returning to each other, takes place? Is this what we are doing right now?

WO: There is no set time. Generally, people come to the realization that they are a part of something bigger, beyond their ego, when they're in the later stages of their lives, having established themselves (proven to others and finally to themselves that they're OK, worthy), but it's not just a matter of reaching a certain point in their career, a fancy title, although many think it is, or attaining a certain amount of money, or some outside influence. These outside recognitions are only a means of helping you work the inside of yourself, which is where most of your judgments lie about how worthy or unworthy you are. Many people actually don't reach this point of confluence in this lifetime and must continue the process wherever their soul goes after they move on from this earthly reality.

E: Is this what's happening to us, to you and me? Are we co-joining?

WO: We have been on this path for many, many years, but it has been sporadic. We really made a breakthrough when you and your small reading group studied the book *Emergence, The Journey from Ego to Essence*, by Barbara Marx Hubbard. And now, as we write this book, we are really cementing the common thinking we have been practicing for these last few years. But the real breakthrough came when you accepted yourself. When you accepted yourself, loved yourself, that's when we really did start coming together.

E: I don't recall any momentous flash of light that announced that event. How or when did that happen?

WO: It was a gradual progression. From ego confidence, and the raising of your own consciousness, to general maturity, moving from the physical teens, 20s, and 30s, to the mental 30s, 40s and 50s, to the spiritual 50s, 60s, and on.

You were staying with your friends in England, Peter and Prue. You were on a different time clock and you sat up chatting until way past midnight. Peter had faded and gone to bed. Prue asked you, out of the blue, "Rob, what's your secret?" It took you by surprise, and you had to think for a while then you answered, "I think my secret is that I totally accept myself, warts and all." That was a conscious moment of realization. You were about 50 at the time.

Where do you want to go with this book?

E: With your help, I want to see what I know. I have some questions about war and peace. Can we break out of this continuous cycle of war? Then there's the question: "What's it all about?" I'm talking about life. Is there something beyond ego gratification, because when you don't have to prove yourself to anyone, not even yourself, what's the point? Is there a point? When the striving stops, it's almost as if, as my friend Karen puts it, "It's empty and meaningless." Are we here just to procreate the next generation for the next bloody war? There's a sadness in me that says this could be the case, that all I've striven for could end up negated by another flag-draped coffin.

I have been at the end of my rope before. The two times that stand out were both about being totally out of money, with no apparent way out. How was I going to feed my family? That was the big responsibility. The contemplation of failure, of ending it all, of giving up, was so real that I was saved only by a visitation, a voice and presence so powerful in its utterance, "Keep going," that there was no question that I wouldn't. I am now realizing that this was you, my wise soul self that gets to be heard when the ego monkey mind chatter finally ceases.

But this time it's different. Money is not the issue, the kids are grown; it's not a question of responsibility. When I had that massive staph infection, for five days before I saw the doctor and it was diagnosed, I lay there not able to pick up a pencil. Like the living dead, all sensation, urgings, ambitions ceased, and I saw the other side, beyond the ego. Life now sometimes seems empty and meaningless. It really brings me back to "What's the point?"

WO:   The important thing for you, if you are feeling adrift, without purpose, what you are calling "what's the point?" is to become clear again. Once you have regained your clarity and purpose we can deal with war and peace.

E:   OK. That makes sense.

## Meditate in Malawi or Sit and Fish on the Banks of the Zambezi

WO: When you ask "What's the point?" you are also asking what's my "purpose"? There is only a point or purpose to life, if you want a point or purpose. You are feeling the diminution of worldly goals, the human tiredness of having struggled for so long, and the consequent question, is it going to be just more of the same? This point in time is a life-changing transition, a whole new arena of consciousness very different from your old pedal-to-the-metal, make-it-happen, never-give-up, driven self, and hence it feels discombobulating because it's unfamiliar and very uncomfortable. Being uncomfortable is a required state for personal growth to occur. You have done some marvelous internal work, yet there is more to do, particularly in the area of surrender.

E: Does this mean I have to give up pleasures like working on my vintage cars, which brings me such peaceful joy but is a very selfish pursuit?

WO: Of course not. We are not about to become monks. Everyone chooses a different path and yours is much more in the public economic arena. Now you could, if you wanted, go and meditate in Malawi or sit and fish on the banks of the Zambezi, both places that you always think about when you want to escape this over-stimulated, over-distracting, money-centric rat race. It's entirely up to you, but there is nothing to stop you having human ego goals. We are talking about our integration here, you and me; therefore, it's a mixture of ego goals and soul goals, if we are to *be* something and also *do* something.

E: So this isn't about elimination of the ego completely, the death of my ego?

WO: It could be. But it's really about integration to a whole new level of consciousness. In a way it is a death because that is the process of life; birth and death, death and birth, and this process causes the death of the old and the birth of the new. While we are living in this reality of Planet Earth, in this electric universe, there is always duality: hot/cold, night/day, male/female. If you were to eliminate one side of the coin, in this case the ego, to achieve what you think the outcome ought to be, it's a form of coercion. We are talking about dissolving and devolving the two sides, ego and soul, into one, for eventual repatriation to the whole, the one still light of Universal Intelligence.

You are at a very interesting juncture. You are moving away from the constant desire of ego to control, into the realm of flow, going with the river instead of paddling against it. The question is then: Do you want to continue with this conversation and all that it entails, or do you want to go fish on the banks of the Zambezi?

E: I want to deal with this war and peace issue.

WO: So, are you now clear that your purpose is to write this book?

E: Yes. Is attaining inner peace a necessary prerequisite for peace in the world?

WO: Yes and no. If a growing number of people cultivated peace within, then you would find that they would have a tremendous influence on world leadership, which could make a huge difference between having peace and having war. You could also have people who don't necessarily practice inner peace on a regular basis but who want peace. For instance, if enough people stopped to pray for peace, it could make a big difference in the way the world operates.

E: Lots of different sects pray for peace with, "If only you could let our side win." This was quite evident during World War I and World War II, where the majority of people fighting were Christian. Each side prayed for victory over the other, as if Universal Intelligence actually chose sides. Does Universal Intelligence choose sides?

WO: Absolutely not! War is a human condition, created by humans, and has nothing to do with Universal Intelligence. Universal Intelligence created the Universe and gave us free will, allowing humans the path of war if they so choose. Let's talk about the causes that humans use to rationalize war, if you like. Because when you know the causes you can address the problems rather than the symptoms. It's all in how we think.

E: Yes, I'd like that. Are these causes separate from the human condition?

WO: No, they are very much part of the beliefs that humans hold. The belief, for instance, that there isn't *enough*, that there is only so much oil, energy, money, water, copper, or labor and you had better get your share before the others get it, even if it means you have to fight over it.

E: But many of these commodities are exhaustible.

WO: Necessity is the mother of invention; isn't that a well-known phrase? Of course there is only so much oil or copper or water, but what's not limited is human creativeness and inventiveness. It's about where you put your attention. Do you put it on fighting over those diminishing resources, wasting all that blood and treasure, or do you put your focus on creating a new form of sustainable eco-friendly technology?

E: It's a strategic decision about where you put your focus?

WO: Yes, and that requires leadership, because as soon as you declare a goal, no matter how small or how large, all sorts of obstacles will begin to show up to test your resolve. This is where human will comes into play. Those leading the charge in this new direction have engaged the positive side of their ego and they are able to tap into their intuition to get inspiration, guidance, and creative insight from their own inner wisdom.

How many stories have you heard of people struggling to invent something new? They wake up in the middle of the night with this great idea or solution to a problem. Why? Because their conscious mind was asleep, allowing their wisdom to speak to them, either in a dream or just as they emerge from sleep. Einstein got his solution to relativity while walking around a lake talking to a colleague about something completely different. Suddenly the solution he had been struggling to find popped into his head.

Let me explain the two sides of ego as I see it from my position deep down inside of you. It looks like two talking heads joined at the neck constantly debating what to do, when to do it, and how to do it. Hence the term used by others: monkey mind chatter.

The positive happy side that loves a challenge says, "Let's move to a new location and start a business."

The fearful side says, "No, no, you can't do that; you'll miss all your family and friends, you'll have no support, you won't know anyone. What if you fail? You'll have to come back with your tail between your legs. What will people think of you?"

Positive side interrupts: "I don't care, I'd rather give it a try (nothing ventured nothing gained) than continue to exist in this crappy job going nowhere."

Fearful side: "You know you are not smart enough, you don't have enough money, etc."

This goes on all the time, the babble inside the head. It's no wonder very few people ever tap into their true wise selves, they seldom if ever have quiet, still, minds.

E: I remember the day the four senior members of our company in South Africa decided we would move to Canada and that I would be the first to go. I drove home that evening with trepidation and excitement. Maggie and I had talked lightly about the possibility of moving, but nothing concrete. As I waited for her to return home from yoga class, I suddenly realized the gravity of the move, so I meditated. When I was sufficiently calm I asked, "Should we move to Canada?" Before the question was fully complete the voice (which I now know as you) physically convulsed my whole body with a resounding "Yes!"

WO:   When you quiet the mind I am always here to guide you, and it doesn't have to be only with the big decisions; it can become a daily moment-by-moment habit.

E:   I know how important understanding the two modes of thinking has been for my own development, and how using *Slowing Down to the Speed of Life* by Richard Carlson and Joseph Bailey with my clients has helped them enormously in their very stressful, superfast-paced world.

WO:   Carlson and Bailey call these modes Process Thinking and Flow Thinking. They really relate to the two states of ego we have been talking about: the fearful state and the happy state. When you are in the fearless state, you are in the Flow, your thoughts are fresh, unencumbered by past memories, creative and fertile, and you can use the positive side of Process Thinking—our analytical, mathematical, logical left brain—at the same time, giving you full use of your thinking powers and the subsequent feelings of enthusiasm and accomplishment.

It is also the time when you are open to hearing the still, small voice within, which often comes through as a fresh insight. You, Rob, know this personally as my voice, your Wise One, because you are now conscious of this connection. Still, there are occasions when you lose it, like all humans, by getting your knickers in a knot over some perceived ego threat.

E: I know I get caught up at times, particularly with those closest to me.

WO: The big thing to remember is that being in Flow mode is natural. All you need to do is watch young kids at play. Although they can get pushy and bossy or cry and retreat from time to time, most of the time they are happy and excited and frequently talking to their imaginary friends, just like you are talking to me. It's the natural state. Now along comes a situation or person that squashes this natural joy. For a child it might be a bigger, stronger kid, a bully, who is seeking to prove himself and solidify his own self-worth in a destructive way, through threat or force. This causes the fearful side to take over, which makes us defensive, and we either fight or flee. The incident can also cause the defensive child to harbor thoughts of resentment and possibly revenge, which, if not let go of at some stage, can cause maladjusted behavior in the future.

E: I've often seen this in a management situation. A group is working well on a project and along comes a more senior person carrying the stick of authority. For no good reason other than to prove himself, he interrupts and treats people badly, resulting in poor morale, resentment, and lower productivity.

WO: Flow Thinking is, as we have said, our natural state and uses both the thought modes. Naturally, it is more efficient and effective than just using the left brain process mode. If, for example, you are designing a new product, say a light switch, you calculate the strength of the material required to withstand the flow of electricity that needs to go through it. You are using the Process Thinking mode, the calculating mind, to do this while also contemplating new ways to design the look and feel, which is more in the creative, aesthetic mode. The two modes happily co-exist in Flow Thinking mode.

The problem comes when your fearful side pops up and asks you questions or makes statements such as, "You're never going to get this done on time. You had better hurry, cut corners, otherwise your boss will get angry and you won't get your bonus," or, "This is beyond your capability. You're going to fail and look foolish in front of other people." In other words, your fearful, critical side intervenes because it is scared.

This is a self-inflicted scenario. The other scenario is when someone comes along and tells you that it's all wrong and you'd better fix it by tomorrow. This can also start up the internal negative conversation. Whatever the external situation is that causes stress, it's what you do with it internally that really matters.

E: I know from my own experience that I've felt hurt by an accusation that someone close to me has made. It's very easy for me to go down the rat hole of circular thinking, going over and over the conversation, and trying every which way to defend my side of the story. Why does it only seem to happen these days with those really close to me, as with my brother when I was in South Africa?

WO: Well that's a perfect example. Your brother was operating in negative Process mode. He was really scared about his middle child who was smoking dope and, in your brother's mind, probably doing other drugs. The boy, who had just turned 18, wanted to go overseas to work in London. Having spoken to the boy, you suggested, from a much more objective view point, that this might be just what he needed to change his environment and get a fresh start.

Your brother was really scared that the boy would get into bad company, take an overdose, and die. He was having a full-blown negative thought attack, and when you made your recommendation, it overflowed his stress bucket. He attacked you for treating it flippantly, which, of course, was something purely in his mind. Being attacked by someone you love, your fearful side got angry and attacked back. Pretty easy to dissect afterwards, but not easy to deal with in the moment. Tell me, why did you apologize the next day?

E: By then I saw it for what it was. My brother was really scared, and having been there myself, I felt tremendous compassion for him and the torture he was going through. I knew he was in no state to apologize for his initial attack, as he was still caught up in the ongoing everyday problem of dealing with this difficult child. I felt that it might help if I apologized (because I could) for attacking back. Apologizing, even if you think the other person started it, will often decrease and release the stress in the situation and some movement forward can be made, if not at that particular point in time then at least, as was the case with my brother, some time later.

WO: This goes back to what we have discussed before. It's all about ego wanting to be right. Ego is so scared that if it's not right it will be punished, like it was as a child. You go into circular process thinking: going over the situation, blaming the other person, trying to defend yourself. This is being defensive, and is why we have a long history of fighting one another.

So the personal pathway is first and foremost to be honest.

This doesn't require the ego to be silent. Ego knows when it is being honest or manipulative, what is right and what's wrong; therefore, nothing more is required than to make a personal dedication that from now on I will be honest and trustworthy in all my dealings.

Second, it is to give up rationalizing violence, both personally and as a nation. All right by might leads only to further destruction.

Let's look briefly at human history and why people fight.

## CHAPTER 2

# THE PAST

WO:  When humans seek to prove themselves through the use of power, it is usually for the purpose of maintaining control, because by maintaining control their fearful ego side thinks they will be safe. This self preservation instinct can be quite helpful in alerting us to danger, but it can also become a problem when the person creates imaginary danger where there is none because that person has becomes stuck in his or her fearful thinking mode.

This is part of the ego's journey. It has been a long trail from caveman to the present, and human experience tells us that this journey is anything but safe.

E:  Human history is a very small fragment of planetary time and it has been a hard struggle for survival. We tend to forget this in our modern-day world of driving to the supermarket to buy whatever food takes our fancy. Of course, there are still plenty of places in the Third World where people scrabble daily for food and water. So why is it such a strong, instinctive urge in us to do almost anything, including killing other humans, to survive?

WO:  Our drive to survive is based in the creative force that lives in every single living thing. Universal Intelligence endowed every single cell with the ability to replicate and evolve. Anything less would have resulted in a static, dead, non-evolving piece of scenery. Thus the purpose of every living thing is to recreate itself through offspring as a part of overall creation.

Humans take this creative urge beyond the desire to replicate themselves, into the realm of creativity which includes the arts, literature, tools, inventions, and machines, all an outgrowth of the basic creation or creative urge endowed within us by Universal Intelligence.

E: Does this mean that the universe will collaborate with our thoughts, desires, and actions?

WO: Yes, to the extent of the strength of those thoughts, desires, and actions; in the respect that it, the universe, is energy, and thoughts are energy, the universe must therefore respond. What you put out, you get back. It's cause and effect. Put out love and respect and you will get it in return. Put out hate and hurt and you will get that in return. This is one reason all "right by might" dictatorships or empires eventually fall. The endgame of ambition through force and destruction can only lead to destruction. This is why love will always endure; its endgame is more love.

E: If Universal Intelligence is love, why are such things allowed?

WO: Universal Intelligence doesn't allow or disallow anything. The system is set up for maximum creative expression that can only be realized with free will. Without free will, Universal Intelligence's purpose would be akin to playing with a model railway, where everything is decided ahead of time, what goes where and for how long, placing the people, animals, and houses wherever desired and making the trains go and stop at will. Very boring and totally noncreative.

No, the universe is set up for infinite possibilities with one proviso: everything must be in balance.

What I'm calling balance, you know as action and consequences. Every time you do something (action) there is a consequence. Remember that time you were heading south toward Denver on the freeway and the road was a sheet of ice? You were driving at five to ten miles per hour when you were passed by a vehicle going much faster and your immediate thought was, "There's an accident waiting to happen." Not ten miles down the road you saw the car upside down in the median. This is an example of the effect being closely related in time to the cause, but not all effects are so immediate.

You know from personal experience that when starting a business, you put in enormous amounts of time, energy, and capital long before you see the fruits of your labor. The same is true of your thinking. If you continue to think positive thoughts, which cause you to act in a positive manner, you will reap positive results. The same is true of negative thinking. Universal Intelligence has set up the universe to be impartial; it returns to you what you put out and that's what I mean by balance. Hate begets hate, violence begets violence, and love begets love.

So let us get back to the question you asked: "Why is it such a strong, instinctive urge in us to do almost anything, including killing other humans, to survive?"

As I mentioned before, it's been a long journey from caveman to the present. While we have the trappings of a modern, sophisticated society, our natural instincts, learned over many centuries, are to fight for and keep resources.

E: And, with our growing populations and diminishing resources, not just oil, but real basics such as food and water, the potential for another world conflict is enormous.

WO: So what we are looking for is a cultural change that takes us from our animalistic past to a more enlightened cooperative world.

E: Is it possible?

WO: We will never know unless we try.

E: If we are going to have an influence on the many human cultures, we need to look at how we got here.

WO: Our human history has been dominated by our hunter gatherer past, and while some recent evidence suggest groups may have gathered in small towns where there was a rich food environment, it is only recently that we turned to agriculture for our means of survival, so much of our instinctual behavior comes from this very scary, unpredictable form of survival that existed prior to our taking up the plow.

For men, physical strength, toughness, and courage in the face of life-threatening dangers developed so that the band of hunters could track down and kill its prey. Leaving the relative safety of the group's *boma* (resting place), the men would set forth in their constant search for food and water. They developed the amazing ability to go for days without food, sometimes without water, and if they were successful, kill, butcher, and find their way back with the harvest. All this time they battled heat and cold, wind and rain, as well as the ever-present danger of wild animals that saw them as prey. Other humans from competing groups or tribes were also a danger. These tribes would willingly kill them in order to protect their own territory and acquire the spoils of the fight. Is it any different today? It's all about the spoils of the fight, be it oil or ideology.

The more skilled, proficient (effective at problem solving), tough, and strong a leader was, the better chance his group had to survive. Within the group itself, he faced competition for the leadership, because to the leader went the spoils, namely the choice of whom and how many wives, and the developing ego pride of being in charge. The skill set then was defined by the need to provide, protect, and produce both food and offspring. The genetic imperative, that built-in creative force for replication, endowed by the Creator in all living things, becomes bundled up in a series of requirements for the leader's own personal, familial, and tribal survival. Nature's great biological adaptation for all this to happen in men goes by the name of testosterone—large, powerful quantities of it. We know women have it as well, but the issue here is quantity. After millions of years of adventure by necessity, it's not hard to see why men crave some risk-taking adventure in today's more mundane life; it's in the blood.

### The Three Fs

WO: In simple terms, the role of men can be defined by the Three Fs.

- Food: And any resource, including territory, oil, or minerals that can stabilize and ensure the flow of food.
- Fight: Size and strength, both personal and in groups; weapons, skill, and determination.
- These first two are for the support of the third, the overriding genetic imperative.
- Future: The very will of nature that causes us to seek whatever solutions necessary to procreate future generations for the survival of the species.

So perhaps it's time to look at our present behaviors and assess whether they are leading us toward that survival or toward the destruction of the species, which I suppose brings us back to looking at the systems that drive behavior. This testosterone-driven behavior, absolutely necessary in the past for the survival of the human race, has created a system based on what many men traditionally are driven by and know how to do: fight and compete. As we have gone from small bands, to tribes, to nation-states, we've found it necessary to make alliances with other nations that share some of our values in order to compete successfully against those that do not.

E: The result of World War II is a good example of forming alliances. The former Axis powers are now aligned in what we call the western industrial society model, or capitalism. And capitalism's success (win) over Communism has served to deepen the West's conviction that it's the only way to go, the only really successful model, that Economic Darwinism will have the last word: only the tough, the most driven, the most competitive will survive. And given the way we've set it up, it's the correct assumption. For those successful at this game, the material benefits are many. But there's also a cost. The standard of living and the quality of life are constantly eroding because competition always demands that we do more with less, i.e., more production, with fewer people, leading to longer working hours and less family time. I think the bigger issue though is the competition for resources.

WO:  You have touched on two of the three Fs: Food, (any resource) and Fight. In the western world model, now emulated by more and more countries, such as India and China, the civilized equivalent of Fight has become capitalism, a system of business that is predicated on competing and winning. The uncivilized version is war.

E:    Capitalism mimics the way we've behaved through our progression out of the jungle.  First, we fight for our piece of turf. In ancient times, this was our tribal boundary. The Bosnian war was a perfect modern-day equivalent, as is the current conflict in the Sudan (despite its splitting into two countries), or the competing warlords in Afghanistan. In the business world, we call it the drive for market share. The second thing we do is consolidate our base and build a defense capability that can ensure our survival. If we can't be the biggest and strongest, we align ourselves with a power we think will succeed, like NATO. The business equivalents are mergers and acquisitions or joint ventures. All this is our drive for survival so that we may pass on our genes to the next generation, what we are calling "Future." Is this tremendous competitive drive by men who are prepared to go to war over territory and resources securing the world for the future, or is it actually making the survival of the planet and the human race more precarious?

Many men don't see anything wrong with the system (the overly competitive winner-take-all mentality); it is what it is. Yet the planet is facing a dire future if we don't do something differently from the past, otherwise it's the old Einstein definition of insanity: doing the same thing over and over again and expecting different results.

I have met many thinking men who are tired of the out-and-out competition, realizing that the end game of Fight is destruction. One of the biggest factors working against peace is that the system we have created, free-market-capitalism, though extremely efficient and powerful at creating wealth, and capable of raising the level of productivity and income of whole nations, is a male stone-age system. This was amply demonstrated by the 2008 financial crash. Financial trading, bundling, derivatives, betting, all greedily seeking the biggest financial return without thought, concern, or knowledge of the outcome, showed the basic atavistic nature of man.

Raw capitalism, like the skills developed by men over the millennia, has been very useful in our development and success up to this point. But the world has changed in the last 100 years more than all the previous centuries put together. We are now facing threats (depletion of global resources and environmental degradation) that this system-raw competitiveness-has exacerbated.

WO:  So you are not advocating a return to some form of socialism/communism?

E:   Definitely not. This isn't about removing competition; it's about evolving so that we don't suffer the destruction of over-competition.

WO: What do you mean by that?

E: Over-competition comes about when you have a limited resource, such as oil, that you're prepared to compete (fight) over instead of seeking a cooperative solution. This could be sharing the development, knowledge, and costs of a new alternative energy methodology that will eventually be good for everyone. It's interesting that the only real multinational development effort is the International Space Station. Why can't we talk to China and others and put our minds and money together to produce what we all need?

WO: You are talking about evolving capitalism.

E: Yes, where we take the best of capitalism's drive, entrepreneurialism, and efficient production and match it with measuring not just the financial bottom line but the social and environmental bottom lines as well.[2]

When we do this in the context of cooperating with other countries for benefit of the planet, we all win.

---

2. Quote by Hazel Henderson: "The financial crisis of 2008 presents the best opportunity in over a century to simultaneously reform money systems and create additional mediums of exchange and financing mechanisms to accelerate the shift from the fossil-fuel/nuclear-Industrial Era to the greener information-rich Solar Age. Today's convergence of global warming, financial crisis and the growing green economy signify a new stage in human awareness and understanding of our place in Nature and are fueling the needed paradigm shift to the Solar Age." (founder of Ethical Markets Media, www.ethicalmarkets.com; author of The Politics of the Solar Age, Doubleday, 1981).

WO: Are you ready to move forward?

E: Yes, let's look at the subject of war and what you and I can do to help bring about a more peaceful world.

## CHAPTER 3

# SCENARIO PLANNING

WO: What the United States could use is a new beginning, a new vision, a new policy. It needs to be demonstrated by bold new behaviors at home, by showing our willingness to be a partner for peace versus a force for bullying, and it needs to be based on the principle that one can only change one's self, and through that, influence change in others. This, of course, requires that others see the United States as strong, because if other countries perceive America as weak, they will (an unfortunate part of ego human behavior) seek to take advantage. Therefore, the first priority is for the United States to get its financial house in order.

E: To do this we need to stop this fractious animosity between right and left. A country divided will fall. It's time to stop the blame game. I call it the "Bastard Syndrome." Blame, accuse, spin, twist, affront, resist, denigrate. These are the base emotions of human consciousness that inflame people to join one side or the other so they can claim "I'm righter" than you. It is the oldest way to gain followers to your way of thinking, but without reasoned discourse at a higher level, the country heads towards greater and greater polarization and "Bastardization," ending in ruination. We are on this slippery slope. Do we still have the quintessential American entrepreneurship to reinvent ourselves?

WO: If we in the United States were to engage in a new, open policy and in new demonstrated behaviors (for example, working with the international community on a full-scale thrust to persuade Israel to return to its pre-1967 borders with fully agreed land swaps with the Palestinians, and the Palestinians to recognize Israel and the path to peace and prosperity through investment), we could even engage with the Iranians and offer, with the rest of the international community, benefits that could sway public opinion. Despite the current religious-based control in their nation, millions of Iranians have demonstrated for a more open, economically viable society. What do we have to lose? In the current situation, neither Israel nor Palestine is safe. The Iranian situation vies with that of Pakistan as the most dangerous in the world, but it requires the major players, starting with the UN Security Council, Russia, China, Britain, France, and the United States, to be of one resolve when it comes to solving these difficult problems.

If we humans don't change our thinking and our approach, it could lead to a major Middle East, or world, conflict. All it takes is thinking differently - and leadership.

WO:  Let us take possibly the most dangerous foreign policy situation in the short-term, the Iran nuclear issue, (although it is possible Pakistan may be even more dangerous) and the most dangerous situation in the middle-term, environmental degradation, desertification, and climate change, both of which carry the capacity for serious, if not total human elimination.

E:     You think that the Iran issue is more important than the environment? Why?

WO:  Because a potential nuclear exchange will alter the current precarious environmental balance beyond our ability to restore it. First, with the geopolitical fallout, cooperation, which is necessary for any real global environmental restoration, will be almost nonexistent. Second, commercial disruption will be massive, and when the economy suffers, so too does the environment. Anger and angst on both sides of the conflict, together with empty bellies, will mean short-term survival takes precedence over long-term care of the planet. If you can get the major powers to cooperate on the nuclear issue, it can also lead to cooperation on the environmental issue.

We cannot predict the future, because people can change their minds at any time. We can, however, be quite prescient if we are observing a trend that does not seem likely to change.

The impasse with Iran is fairly predictable (ending with a really bad result) if we don't succeed in influencing them to become a part of the world community. First, we need Russia and China, together with the other members of the Security Council, to be partners for peace.

E:   If the major powers were to come together we could, as they say, make an offer the Iranians couldn't refuse. First, the offer would have to be genuine. Second, it would have to be big, bold, and bountiful. Third, it would have to be a broad coalition of the international community. Fourth, it would have to have ironclad security guarantees for Iran. Fifth, it would have to hold guarantees of no outside interference on how they run their country. All this would be in the context of Iran foregoing its nuclear program and violent rhetoric. If this were made known publicly, then even in a repressed news state like Iran, given the Internet and satellite TV, the news would spread rapidly. It would then be up to the Iranian people, many of whom have already demonstrated their desire for change. They have seen both success and oppression with the Arab Spring and one day that spring will turn into summer.

WO: We need to look at some scenarios that might shed some insight on our future direction. Given the current trends, it is possible to extrapolate the possible future course of events with scenarios, but I must remind you again that anything can change in a moment if people change their thinking. The Universal Law of Attraction states that you will manifest that which you think, individually and collectively. Therefore, all we are doing is taking what we see as the current state of current thought and seeing where that might lead us.

E: What's the worst case and what's the best case?

WO: I think we need to put forth a few possible scenarios of how the worst case may come about, then work backwards to see if we can put forward a different course of action that would bring about the opposite result.

I am usually low key and somewhat understated but, please don't underestimate the dire seriousness facing the human race.

### Possible Nuclear War Scenario One

WO: Iran: If there is a continuation of this pursuit to gain nuclear weapons and to eliminate Israel, then at the first sign of a real threat or attack by Iran, Israel will simply attack with a nuclear bomb.

E: There are many Iranians who want a different form of governance and they have expressed themselves in the streets, but will it be enough?

WO: Imagine a nuclear explosion 100 times more powerful than Hiroshima and Nagasaki put together. If nothing else happened, if Pakistan didn't get in on the act, if North Korea didn't take advantage and strike Japan, if India didn't take advantage and invade the disputed territories of Kashmir, if China didn't react, if Russia didn't react, if none of these things happened, can you still imagine the effects on the world financial markets? Stock markets would collapse, currencies would collapse, real estate values would collapse. The world economy would be in total disarray, far exceeding the 2008 financial meltdown.

E: And when financial chaos ensues, governments see no way out but to distract the population with a threat from outside, which leads to war.

### Possible Nuclear War Scenario Two

WO: Pakistan is an extremely complicated situation that presents no easy solution. It is not just the extremist against the elected government. They lack a viable economy. The military holds tremendous influence in commercial business as a result of handouts by ex-President Musharraf and his ilk. The military and the secret service favor certain extremist groups, which complicates the ability of the Pakistan government to rein them in. The Northwest Territories are historically ungovernable, being fiercely tribal in nature.

Afghanistan is on one side of the country and India on the other, with the disputed territory of Kashmir always providing the immediate trigger point.

Should Pakistan destabilize even further from civil war to another military coup, who knows what the regional response might be?

India, fed up with Pakistan-based terrorists bombing India, could use the power vacuum as an opportunity for military action.

Pakistan, through use of its own nuclear capability, could threaten India and drag them into a conflict, causing a domino effect whereby the West is drawn in and China feels threatened. China sees an opportunity and takes advantage of the situation to exact huge concessions, or in the worst case, attacks neighboring countries while everyone is distracted.

The scenarios increase should Pakistan fall into the hands of these extremists. Iran is opposed to the Sunni movements in Pakistan (remember Iran fought an eight year war with Sunni-led Iraq), including those of the Taliban and Al-Qaeda, and is scared of Pakistan's nuclear capability, which gives Iran yet another reason to have its own nuclear weapons. It is quite possible, though improbable at this time, that these two countries could face off, drawing the whole region and the West into a real nuclear nightmare.

E:   This doesn't seem to leave us with many options in Pakistan except to support the civilian government with the emphasis on helping developing the economy.

### Possible Nuclear War Scenario Three

E: Hezbollah/Hamas and its backers (Iran and others) incite further chaos in Palestine and Israel, causing the Israeli army not to hold back this time, causing Iran not to hold back, causing the nuclear first strike by Israel against Iran, causing militant Muslim uprisings throughout the world, causing the overthrow of the democratic government of Pakistan, which uses its nuclear capability, causing the escalation of nuclear war. Turmoil like this is the goal of the military side of Islamic extremism and is a threat not just to the West but also China, Russia, and the world.

WO: While the situation in Iran may be the most dangerous, it is inextricably linked to the Israeli-Palestinian conflict through, as you mention, Iran's backing of the militant factions who want to see Israel wiped from the map. When you put scenarios One and Three together, you have the loose, dry gunpowder to ignite the nuclear keg.

### Possible War Scenario Four

E: The Middle Eastern regional countries align into Sunni versus Shiite, a form of civil war, escalating the Iraq situation, which then spills over into neighboring countries, causing turmoil and widespread destruction of oil-producing equipment. This causes worldwide oil shortages, economic recession/depression, and western anger and retaliation, leading to the drafting into the military of ordinary men and women to fight a growing global war, further bankrupting the treasuries of western countries.

### Possible War Scenario Five

WO: Any serious disruption of the world's oil supply over the next 20 years (or until the world has some measure of independence from this energy source) will cause a major economic meltdown. When enough people are out of a job, when enough money has been expunged from the world's capital markets, when the duly elected governments (I include Russia and China in this scenario) are hanging by a thread and don't know what to do, it bears repeating: they will do what governments have done historically when things are not going so well at home. They will go to war in distant lands to consolidate their people against the perceived outside threat.

E: Japan's big fear in the late 1930s was lack of oil, which finally led them to attack the United States at Pearl Harbor on December 7th, 1941. Hitler marched into Russia and headed for the Russian oil fields and thus ensued the battle for Stalingrad. Neither turned out well for either country in the long run, but it shows what nations are prepared to do if they lack a certain essential resource.

### Possible War Scenario Six

E: Collapse from within. The typical ebb and flow business cycle is exacerbated this time by some unusual factors. The sub-prime lending fiasco has an indeterminate bottom. Nobody knows when the last shoe will drop or the last stone be upturned. This unfathomable hole has already caused massive losses and once blue-chip companies, e.g., Bear Stearns, to be sold off for pennies on the dollar. Combine this with the ordinary citizen being overstretched and in debt with a falling asset base (houses, stocks, wages and jobs declining), and with exactly the same situation for the government, and you have the recipe for collapse.

How can the government of the richest nation on earth be vulnerable to financial collapse? When you issue paper money or electronic money, its value is based on confidence in the issuing authority, i.e., the government. When that body continues to run up debt (more expenses than income), eventually it has to pay the piper. The piper(s) in this case are foreign governments sitting on billions of dollars of United States currency, watching their once-safe assets crumble and wondering, should we keep buying more of the same or should we cut our losses and cash in? The more the dollar falls, the more the price of oil rises. The more oil rises, the more the dollar falls. A vicious, spiraling down-cycle that is extremely difficult to stop when it is all based on subjective confidence. The opposite gyration is when people in other countries shift their capital out of their countries' currencies into the dollar because they perceive it to be safer. The dollar then rises, masking the underlying problem of deteriorating confidence in United States paper currency.

The costs of two wars, the interventions by the government, billions for stimulus packages, massive injections of liquidity into teetering banks, insurance companies, Fannie Mae, Freddie Mac and the auto industry, interest rate drops and Quantitative Easing (a fancy name dreamed up to fool the public that means nothing more than printing/creating money out of nothing) by the Federal Reserve Bank all add to a highly probable future of inflation that will turn rampant.

Osama bin Laden and Al-Qaeda might just have been smart enough to realize that the more they draw us into foreign wars, the more we become vulnerable financially.

When the world economic system starts to teeter, everyone gets scared, including presidents and prime ministers. Tensions rise, and extremism and national solipsism supplant reason, while the terrorists sit back and watch as the great Satan and democracy destroy themselves through infighting that follows financial ruin.

WO:   Many people have commented on this, and the American People are tired of the flaccid, feckless inability of the two parties to come to grips with the real problem and make things happen. All they seem capable of is blaming each other.

### Possible War Scenario Seven

WO:   The terrorist nuclear bomb attack. Whether the bomb or bombs are set off here in the United States or in some other country, it will be the terrorist objective to start a retaliatory response by the United States. This will inevitably draw in China or Russia, or both, possibly opposing such action and cause the major powers to fight amongst themselves, escalating the conflict beyond all reason and diplomacy.

E:     Having lived and worked in eight counties I have seen how quickly leaders can turn from reasonableness to attack.

WO:   And years later, nobody quite remembers why. An example closer to home is Vietnam. We are now doing business where once we were fighting. When will we learn? Right by might never works.

**Possible War scenario Eight**

WO:   All or none of the above. It's impossible to plan for every possible situation, particularly when it's more likely that it will be the unexpected rather than the expected that will cause the wildfire of violence to spread. World War I was started, albeit in a tense situation (just like we have now), by a single extremist (part of the Serbian nationalist movement) running out of the crowd and shooting the Crown Prince of Austria-Hungary. Russia backed the Serbs, seeking to gain influence. Days later, Germany declared war on Russia, starting a domino effect of different countries joining one side or the other. It's estimated that 40 million people (split almost equally between military and civilian) were casualties in The Great War. World War II, which is now being viewed by some as a continuation of World War I, is estimated to have caused over 70 million (46 million civilian, 26 million military) casualties. All because countries were vying for influence over other countries and resources. Is it any different today?

We have barely contained violent brush fires called Iraq, Afghanistan, and Pakistan for which nobody can come up with a solution to put out the flames. The only way to supersede these ideologues is with a different and better idea. We cannot fight our way out like we did in World War I and World War II, as there is no defeating the opposing army as we did with Germany and Japan. There are definite grounds for the argument that the more we fight, the more resistance we create. We need to prioritize the most serious threats and determine what we can do about them.

E: It's our job, the people's job, to tell the government what we want, and there is no doubt in my mind that the greatest internal threat to our own security, and hence to world security, is our complete lack of political ability to face up to reality, and work on sound, long term solutions for dealing with the debt and unemployment.

**CHAPTER 4**

# THE POLITICAL

WO: The current situation of enormous violence in the Middle East has put the world on the slippery slope to all-out war, and American actions in the preemptive attack on Iraq have played a big part in the tenuous situation that now exists. There is plenty of blame to go around. The question is, can that be put aside and the blame game stopped and a new course for peace charted? It's clear that ordinary people of all stripes in all countries are for peace. It is only the fringe elements that are perverting the name of God to justify war. Universal Intelligence never promotes violence as a means of conflict resolution. That is purely a human rationalization. Therefore, it is up to humans to stand together for peace. It is time for the Jews to stand for peace; it is time for the Christians to stand for peace; it is time for the Muslims to stand for peace; it is time for people of every religion and atheists to stand for peace, to stand side by side against the forces of hatred.

E: Are you also indicating there's a shortage of time?

WO: Yes. Our current world situation is unstable and getting worse, not better. The ecological environment is disintegrating and getting worse, not better.

No matter who we elect, that person can never follow through on all his or her promises. The structure (it's always the structure that drives human behavior) of our political system is that once on the inside, the vortex of influence (the money issue again) will suck that person away from what he or she wants to do. The electorate will always be disappointed and further disillusionment with democracy ensues. This creates its own vicious circle of distrust and shows up as extremely low approval ratings for the government. No matter how charismatic the candidates or how solid their backgrounds, they will be stymied by the process unless the people get involved. We need to engage the people to such an extent that the elected leaders really have to follow through on the people's desires. We need to de-emphasize the party system and elect candidates (from both parties and independents) who are prepared to stand first and foremost for the Country.

## CHAPTER 5

# THE PEOPLE

The question at the beginning of the book was:

*How do we the people, without resorting to violence, exert power, so that those in power (the government and the shadowy money influencers who control the politicians) cannot ignore us, dismiss us, or crush us?*

The answer is: Dispersed concentration.

E: If we, the people, can concentrate around the vision, "A Planet at Peace" yet be dispersed across the country and one day around the globe, then we cannot be ignored, dismissed or crushed.

If I were to stop for just one minute and think a peaceful thought, would that help my mood, my attitude, my daily life? Would this one minute inspire my next moment? And, if this moment affects me as an individual, surely it will affect my interaction with others. Do I want peace in my life, in my body, in my mind, in my soul of souls? If I answer yes, then I'm bound to commit to that intention. And if I'm among others who also commit, our peaceful intentions could have a ripple effect throughout the world. It is in the minds of the people that the secret of power lies, not in the hands of one person or an anointed few. Real power is in the creative force of the many, focused on a common goal. The political gulf between the ideologues of the left and right needs to be bridged.

WO: When a gulf or rift appears, just like a vacuum, it begs to be filled. In an orderly society, even though shaken to its financial core, this can be achieved over time, and we can add our voice to the mix of ideas. But none of that will happen if the world turns to confrontation and conflict instead of co-operation. Therefore we must not lose sight of our vision and our mission before we discuss how to get our own financial house in order.

**Vision:** A Planet at Peace

**Mission:** To enlist women and men who will cry out for this vision, and compel their governments to work toward this realization.

**Goal:** The countries of the world to co-operate in presenting an alternative to war by devising a package for peace.

### The Process

*Step 1*

Get the permanent members of the United Nations Security Council, China, France, Russia, the United Kingdom, and the United States, to sit down at a conference for economic cooperation and peace.

**The goal:**

1. An unequivocal Peace Treaty that declares: *"No more war between our nations."*
2. Set up a joint Peace and Cooperation council. All five countries of the Permanent Security Council to be

represented plus some others from the G20. This to be a cabinet position with direct access to the President or Prime Minister.

Their job is to continuously work on the current war issues and potential issues with immediate emphasis on the Middle East, Iran, and Pakistan.

E: I've witnessed such unyielding support for one political side or the other that people don't even listen to the other side's point of view; they just get angry and start shouting. Where did civility and reasoned discourse go?

WO: When enough people get dissatisfied with the pettiness, the mudslinging, and the anything-to-win attitude, the desire for change becomes paramount and opportunity presents itself. Here in America, we have the freedom to demonstrate and call for change, and if enough of us make a stand for peace now, our politicians will get the message. The confluence of the pursuit of "Peace" and "Fiscal Responsibility" gives us the opportunity to come together as Americans and forgo party politics.

The internet, blogosphere, and social media like Facebook have given people the potential to regain their influence over their politicians (think of Egypt) and voice their concerns over the most critical issue facing the planet: nuclear war or peace. People can sign on from anywhere in the world. The purpose is to let the President know that the people are going to hold the executive branch responsible for getting the major heads of state, starting with the members of the Security Council, to come together to design a Package for Peace. That shows:

- That cooperation is the pathway to peace.
- That peace is the pathway to health and planetary health.
- That health is the pathway to wealth and the elimination of poverty.

E: I think it is entirely possible that other countries might start their own Stand for Peace movements.

WO: We are all in this together. Getting major countries talking and cooperating on peace will lead to many other opportunities for dialogue and action on global issues such as the environment. It doesn't take much foresight to realize that if countries cooperate, there can be a panoply of benefits. Imagine a huge nuclear mushroom cloud on the one hand, or a picture of you and your family enjoying peace and financial prosperity on the other hand. It is up to us. If people think, "What's the use? It'll never work," then guess what? We get what we think.

E: Democracy is great until apathy sets in. When only a small portion of the electorate votes, the wisdom of the people is lost. Even if we vote in large numbers, we rarely get the chance to hold our politicians accountable, and so they get four years in which to misbehave.

WO: All we can ask is that people do their bit.

E: The fate of the world lies with us, the people. If we do nothing, then the politicians will do what they've always done: pursue their own political careers for their own ego purposes. We must hold their feet to the fire by being prepared to stand for what we want.

### Some Years Later after the funeral

Not many people are aware of the significance of the $11^{th}$ of November, its origin having slipped away, but veterans know. On the $11^{th}$ hour of the $11^{th}$ day of the $11^{th}$ month in 1918, my grandfather, together with many other bugle players, sounded the *Last Post* in the British lines, as *Taps* was sounded simultaneously along the American lines, signaling the end of World War I. The war, it was said, to end all wars. Yet there we were, Dave and I, almost a century later, attending a Veterans Day memorial service in the small town of Cupertino, California, knowing as we stood there that our troops were currently engaged in two wars.

Matt's parents and wife had worked tirelessly with family, friends, and the town of Cupertino to raise money for the park and a beautiful bronze statue.

The statue was life size and depicted Matt Axelson and his buddy, James Suh, in full combat gear. Both were kneeling in a tactical position watching each other's back. The statue's accuracy and realism made me gulp.

We think of them as supermen, indestructible, but they are not. They are carefully selected, highly trained men of great courage and stamina, men of high intellect and strong morals, men who love life and know how to show respect and compassion.

The Secretary of the Navy got up to speak and said that according to historians, in the last 3,000 years, there have only been 284 days without a war going on somewhere.

After two more speeches, Matt's parents went to the podium to thank everyone for their participation. I had already told my wife, Maggie, that if this ever happened to us (not only Dave, but also our youngest son Mike is a Green Beret medic), she would have to speak because I knew I would not be capable. She told me she didn't think she would be able to either. Donna spoke, her voice cracking. Then she moved to the statue to lay flowers. Her final caress of Matt's hand as if to bring him back to life made my whole body tremble, and I put my hand on Dave's knee to reassure myself.

This had been the most memorable Veterans Day service I had ever attended, not only because of its program, its dignitaries, and its setting, but also because it struck so close to home.

As Dave and I were saying goodbye at the airport, he confided to me that he felt exhausted from the emotional roller coaster, tired from shedding so many tears.

## EPILOGUE

# FINANCIAL MELTDOWN

E: What's the meaning of this financial collapse?

WO: It is the beginning of a new world order. It is what we have been writing about in this book. The reason this book has been written and rewritten a number of times over the years since July 2005 is that the world is changing not just at a rapid pace, but, more importantly, momentously. The financial meltdown is not just a "Great Recession." It signals that the world will never be the same again and that the formulas and prescriptions that have been used in the past will not necessarily work in the future.

But it's as if we were alone with a few others in a darkened, soundproof room knowing in our gut that something was wrong but unable to get anyone's attention. Suddenly a curtain has been ripped asunder and a shaft of cold, hard light has illumined the unfettered folly—the fallacy that somebody knows how to run a global banking system, that unfettered avarice was good for the people, that spending more than we earned was really okay, that using our military force against people we didn't like was really okay when the prize was perceived strategic control over territory and oil.

There is the potential for a big evolutionary jump for humankind, or, conversely, a regression into a dark, dark age.

The beauty of the cold hard light is that it forces people to focus and take action. Until now, the system impounded anyone who called for change into a quarantine of moral impotence. We knew something was wrong but no one wanted to listen. Whoever said the words to the effect that "Capitalism holds the seeds to its own self destruction" must be laughing the hollow laugh of schadenfreude.

What to do in a world turned upside down? We, or any other country, can choose the path to reconstruction, co-operation, peace, and future prosperity, or can be selfish and nationalistic, using this as an excuse to go to war. Every possible war scenario we have written prior to this meltdown is now ten times more likely to occur because people are afraid and don't know what to do. When this happens, people look for direction from their leaders and all too often leaders try to look strong by lashing out.

E: It is obvious that people cannot be trusted with a totally unfettered, unregulated capitalistic system. The atavistic ego greed is simply too much for most people to handle. The growth of the unregulated shadow banking system in the last 20 to 30 years has caused this over-leveraged, over-borrowed house of cards to come tumbling down. Therefore we must put in place simple principles; e.g., if an institution is too big to fail, then it is too big and must be broken up. If a broker, bank, or rating institution is giving advice as to the value (rating) of any company or organization, it must be at arm's length with no monies passing between them. Making 1,000-page documents that specify this rule and that rule only complicates business and provides fertile ground for its subversion. Complication like this is the enemy of the people; we need principles, transparency, and oversight that allow for stable growth and prosperity.

WO: The real problem is that if the United States goes broke, it can only lead to major conflict just like World War II, except this time with nuclear weapons. Therefore, knowing that we do not know all the answers, we can at least start the conversation rolling with some ideas of a financial and political plan that can help turn this travesty around.

E: Most Americans have never lived overseas and have not seen how quickly a country can go from peaceful and prosperous to conflict and collapse. Yes, we have our history of the Civil War, during which this happened, but that was so long ago that most people think that it could never happen again. Zimbabwe, where I grew up, is a case that shows how quickly a country that loses control over its finances can cause major suffering for the ordinary people. I remember my son Mike visiting there in 1997, and, if I recall correctly, he got approximately 12.5 Zimbabwe dollars to one U.S. dollar. When my brother Derek and I visited in 2002, we changed our South African rands (approximately 1 U.S. dollar equaled 10 rand) on our first day there at 360 Zimbabwe dollars to one rand. Five days later we changed again and got 480 to the rand; multiply this by 10 and you get 4,800 Zimbabwe dollars to one U.S, dollar.

We visited an old friend of Derek's who had sold his very successful safari business a couple of years before for the equivalent of several million U.S. dollars but was paid in Zimbabwe dollars. He had already seen his life's work devalued by half but thought it couldn't get any worse. A few years later he had nothing except a lot of useless paper money.

This escalation of inflation continued at an ever growing pace, forcing the government to print ever larger and larger bills. I carry around in my wallet a bill issued in July 2008 for 100 billion Zimbabwe dollars, which soon after it appeared would not buy even a loaf of bread. Economists have estimated that in 2008 the inflation rate was 231 million percent.

When I visited Zimbabwe in April of 2009 I got into conversation with a man called Max, who told me that until they changed the law earlier in the year so that everyone was allowed to deal in "Forex" (foreign exchange), he didn't even bother to go to the bank to collect his wages (paid in Zimbabwe dollars) because by the time he got the money and went to spend it, it had devalued significantly. He was the accountant for a firm that made car springs and had been there for 23 years. His saving grace was he lived in a hut with no electricity, no rent, and his wife grew mealies (corn) to supplement their meager diet of food bought or bartered on the black market.

The black market was how most everyone survived. Nearly everyone had a relative who had fled Zimbabwe seeking work, mainly to South Africa or Botswana. This mass migration of an estimated three to four million adults had caused xenophobic riots and brutal beatings of these "illegal alien African wetbacks," but these émigrés, with their remittances of foreign money, were the saving grace for the families back home. Everyone used the black market, including government officials. It was the only way to survive.

Suddenly, with the lifting of the ban on foreign exchange, Max's wages were paid in a currency that people had confidence in, and almost immediately most everything could be bought in the stores and gas was available at the gas stations again. Moving from Zimbabwe dollars to other, more stable currencies will work for a small country like Zimbabwe, but what happens when the world's major currency fails? There will be no place to turn.

What happened in Zimbabwe is called hyperinflation. I remember stories when I was a young boy of how people in Germany after the First World War had to take a wheelbarrow of money to the store to buy a loaf of bread. As a young boy I thought it was just a story, but it wasn't. It was true, and it led to the disenchantment of the German people so that they looked to a strong leader who could lead them out of their misery, and that leader was Hitler.

Asia, Argentina and Mexico have all had massive financial meltdowns which were saved largely by the U.S. and its surrogates the World Bank and the International Monetary Fund. But what happens when the US dollar goes into hyperinflation and loses its status as the world's reserve currency? Who will save America? What happens when a U.S. Navy ship wants to refuel in some foreign country and that country refuses to take our note because by the time the supplier is paid, the dollar will have sunk in value and the supplier will have lost money? The same will happen when we want to buy commodities such as oil, copper, and iron ore. But the biggest problem will be the breakdown of the food supply. When people get hungry, they realize the government has let them down and they get violent. In Zimbabwe this unrest was fairly easily handled by

President Robert Mugabe's fearsome police and army. The same can be seen in Iran. Will the U.S.government employ the same tactics?

### A New Day in Politics

*If for the most part we elect good, honest people to be our representatives in Washington, then why are we continually disappointed?*

E: I see now the single biggest threat to world peace has now become America's crushing debt, that which has already been incurred and what will continue to be incurred in the future. If we the people do not take control of our monetary process, the politicians will continue their profligate ways and the next (and inevitable) financial collapse will be unstoppable. There will be no stepping back from the cliff this time with the treasury and the Fed bailing out the banks, AIG, GM, Chrysler, Freddie and Fannie Mae and all the others. Why? Because there will be no more money. Even the Federal Reserve will not be able to create money out of thin air with the click of a mouse, as it has already done, because paper money depends on confidence and there will be none. There will be no more bailing out the PIGS of Europe (**P**ortugal, **I**reland, **G**reece and **S**pain) who are already bankrupt, or their keepers, Britain, Italy, Germany, and France; there will be no bailing out the U.S. by the IMF, or the Chinese. Instead there will be civil unrest in the streets, mass anger in countries toward one another followed by WAR, as the governments see it as the only way out of the chaos. Why? Because unlike the the case of the Zimbabwean dollar, which no one cares about, when the US dollar goes, so does every other currency in the world.

WO:   Therefore we need structural change.

E:     There is a growing anger in the country that whatever we do, whichever party we elect, the outcome is the same—petty party politics, petty self interest, all devoured by the money influencers' vortex, ensuring feckless governance.

These "Influencers" love the game that goes on between the Democrats and Republicans because it's a façade that gives people the impression that they (the people) are exercising their democratic right, but it's a shell game, a sham. The emperor, "the two-party system," has no clothes. We need Democracy 2.0, in which we the people take back control.

WO:   Therefore we must look beyond the person, beyond the people we elect, to the structure, systems, and culture that drive ineffective (and often dishonest) behavior. Let me explode a long held myth. The myth is that there is someone out there who understands it all and can lead us out of this mess. There is no one! We have to rely on ourselves.

E:     We need an uprising of the people, who will demand, non-violently, a change in the way of governance so that the people we send to Washington in the future know with absolute certainty that if they do not do the will of the people, they will be thrown out. The new era is not about which party will win; they are both as bad as each other. It is about doing the will of the people, not that of the party. The job of the new electives will be to coalesce around a common set of goals as outlined in a manifesto. Any disdain for such goals will cause the politicians to lose their seats.

WO:   There is no time to form a new third party. We must select new candidates from both Democrats and Republicans who are willing to stand up to the system, stand up for the country, who are not afraid, who have the courage and integrity to say no to the special interests and the money vultures.

E:   While there will never be complete agreement on any platform or manifesto, it is time to concentrate on a few major issues, to put aside our many ideological differences, to come together as a country, Independents, Republican and Democrats, in order to save the country, lest we drown in the swamp of our own corrosive squabbling.

Let us be clear. Everyone has an opinion and everyone thinks that their opinion is right, which of course is impossible. There are only those ideas that can move the conversation forward. Having to be "right" is what causes wars. Anger is only good for moving us out of apathy, but it is not good for creating solutions.

As our friend Alan has outlined, what we need is a structure that allows for the best and brightest from anywhere, even someone from outside of the country, to be brought together in small groups of approximately four to six people to advise each minister. So for example, the Minister of Energy would bring this non-partisan, nonpolitical group of experts together to discuss, deliberate, and make, transparent to the people, recommendations for solving energy issues.

The minister would take this advice and promulgate it through the civil service, instead of what often happens, which is that the minister ends up doing what the civil service wants him or her to do.

This way you can have these small councils of non-politicians (nor must they be trying to become politicians) who have expertise in each area of government, instead of cronies and party hacks who have their own personal career agendas.

Each council group can be taught the "enhanced decision making technique" that leads to far better policies for solving really difficult current and future problems without incurring the all-too-common problem of unintended consequences, which nearly always make matters worse. No politician is using this methodology, and consequently we are making incomplete decisions that come back to haunt us, all the while piling problem upon problem.

WO:  Let's give an example:

The human race has achieved many wonderful technological advances, from the wheel to the computer, by using the core decision-making framework. This framework, involving as it does all conscious actions being directed toward the achievement of an objective, a mission, or a vision, is essentially linear. The race to put a man on the moon is an excellent example. When NASA started they didn't know how they were going to achieve their mission but they pursued a linear, logical process of solving one problem after another until they reached their goal. If you stop to think about it, everything we "make" involves technology in some form and is almost always successful. However if we stop to think of everything we "manage" from governments, to economies, to agricultural production, to natural resources like water, we are running into problems.

Using the core framework for managing complex systems, such as running a country and making policy decisions that affect many spheres of life, nearly always leads to unintended consequences because the goals are too narrow. To overcome this piling up of unintended consequences, we need to use the enhanced holistic framework. The key to this is first and foremost, having a clearly-defined holisticgoal against which we test all our decisions and ask ourselves if any decision we make takes us towards or away from our holisticgoal. Let me give a single one person example:

If a man is in debt for $100,000 and his goal is to get out of debt, he can sell his house, his furniture, his car, his motor bike, and all his other assets and pay off his debt completely. Reaching his goal in this way, however, has negative consequences; he now has nowhere to live and no way to get to work. In essence, he now becomes a social problem, perhaps living in shelters and relying on charity.

If, however, he has a holisticgoal that states:

I want to live a creative, productive, and meaningful life by using my talents to produce income and build a solid financial foundation, which will allow me to pursue those things I desire for a satisfying quality of life—a family, a house, a garden, and time to go mountain biking—and will also make it possible for me to invest in my own business in the future; his goal, which is still to get out of debt, is dealt with in an entirely differently way. He makes a plan to set aside a portion of his income to make regular payments of interest and principle to pay down his debt. If this requires him to give up some luxury items (non-essentials) in his budget, then he must do this until either he earns more and can afford them again, or he has reduced his debt substantially and has more money because of it.

E: If we take this example and expand it to think about a holisticgoal for the country, what is it we want? This of course requires input from many different stakeholders but even without that, we can work with a "generic" holisticgoal because, frankly, it is a rare individual who does not want what most of us desire. Who, for instance, does not want more prosperity? Who does not want more peace? Who does not want a more rewarding and secure family life? Who does not want freedom to pursue their own spiritual/religious beliefs? Who does not want better education and health for their children? Who does not want a more stable and productive environment to sustain their business and their community? Who does not want security in old age?

Even where all stakeholders simply cannot be gathered together, those who formulate policies can hold to a generic holisticgoal for any community or nation and make decisions and take actions that are consistently in line with that holisticgoal. Any holisticgoal at any level is 100 percent what people want and 0 percent how to achieve it. The how-to is subject to decision-making in which many ways of achieving any objective are tested using the guiding light of a holisticgoal. Currently, this is not done because all of us unknowingly use the core framework, i.e., making our decisions and taking action based on objectives and goals alone. Thus, because of conflicting objectives we find that despite our great resource base (the greatest being the creative spirit of the American people), our quality of life is deteriorating and the forms of production (fewer people working to produce something of value) are diminishing, leaving us with less and less income, which means continually increasing the debt and robbing our children of a decent future.

It's become obvious that, given the spiraling debt, which affects every aspect of production as well as our quality of life, we first must make a plan to stop the bleeding (the ever-increasing debt), then set about paying it down. However, as soon as we test this decision against our holisticgoal, which includes peace, prosperity, security, stability and everything we desire, we realize that, just like the one-person example, we can't make a linear goal of selling all our assets and becoming destitute; we must make a strategic plan that allows for the gradual reduction of our debt in order to take into account all aspects of our lives, public and private, social and environmental. If we kill the goose that lays the golden egg (the egg being the American people and their forms of production), this will end up with people rioting, much the same as our single person ends up homeless. In other words, both outcomes result in a social problem—not a solution.

We must increase the forms of production, i.e., the regeneration of the economy, and we do this by tapping into the creative entrepreneurial culture of America.

WO:   Now let us put some of our ideas into the mix, our manifesto, in order to stimulate some new and different thinking, for surely the old ways will not work.

E:

*Issue*

The National Debt!

We have allowed government to keep spending and spending when we do not have the money.

*Possible solution*

If you think of the economy as a human patient, it could be described as a person who is 700 pounds overweight. This is the result of gluttony, overeating, which is the result of overspending and buying on credit. The patient has been doing this for decades with particular encouragement from the brain (government), which continues to think and promulgate that Eat, Eat, Eat, i.e., Spend, Spend, Spend is the de facto way of life with no thought that one day we will have to settle the account.

Suddenly, and not too surprisingly, this vastly overweight patient has had a heart attack. The first responders have administered massive transfusions (of money) to save the patient from dying, but they have not been able to deal with the real issue for long term health: weight reduction!

The two methods of reducing weight and strengthening the heart back to health are to limit intake of food (spending) and to design a healthy exercise program (economic stimulus) that does not spend more borrowed money, but produces money through incentivizing human creativity.

WO: We must be careful not to become grossly austere; reducing the weight of an unhealthy patient too quickly will only exacerbate the problem. Look how long it has taken you to recover your strength through exercise since the radiation, and how long it has taken to shed the extra weight. As your old friend Michael would say, "Things take longer than they do." This requires a long-term strategy, not some political party's tactical solution for winning the next election.

### Weight Reduction Ideas

WO:

*Issue*

Complication is the friend of the money influencers and the enemy of the people.

*Possible solution*

Any bank that is too big to fail must be broken up into smaller banks that cannot bring down the system.

Regulate all retail banks so that they are not allowed to operate in the "gambling" business, i.e., any form of derivative-type business.

Regulate Wall St. so that it cannot overextend itself and threaten the financial system.

Allow private money and private banks to speculate with their own money up to an acceptable limit as a percentage of their liquid holdings.

E:

*Issue*

When there is no law to stop human avarice, the politicians will keep spending, and spending and spending.

*Possible solution*

Pass a balanced budget law now!

Cap all spending at 2008 levels until a review of priorities shows where to cut and where to expand.

Retaining America's credit rating is essential; otherwise we will be forced by the world bond market to pay ever-increasing interest rates that will add to the debt faster than we can cope, even with a good long term repayment plan. This will sink us much like it has sunk the Greeks.

WO:

*Issue*

The military-industrial complex has too much power.

*Possible solution*

Get out of Iraq.

Get out of Afghanistan. While the military leaders are doing their best, it is an un-winnable war. You cannot change the culture of this ancient, tribal, pastoral, feudal society through military might. This is especially true when you are trying to build on a foundation of sand. The government of Karzai is totally corrupt and useless.

We would create far more friends and far fewer enemies if we showed these pastoral people how to greatly increase their farming productivity and at the same time start reversing the increasing desertification that, if not reversed, will destroy all future efforts for a viable economy.[3]

Get out of South Korea. 28,000 plus American troops in South Korea will not stop a million-man North Korean army if it chooses to invade. It would only mean 28,000 plus American casualties. Only a nuclear bomb or the influence of the Chinese will stop the North Korean army.

Get out of Japan. This is old World War II thinking.

Get out of Europe. We are not defending Europe any longer against the Russians.

It may be necessary to keep certain locations for military intelligence and for strategic logistical purposes, but these do not need massive amounts of troops.

One-third of the money saved would go to defending our ports, borders and homeland security. Two-thirds would go to national debt reduction.

---

3. www.savoryinstitute.com.

E:

### Issue

The size of government has continued to grow with every administration, Democratic or Republican.

### Possible solution

Reduce the size of the federal government by 3% per annum until the national debt is paid off completely. This can be done primarily through retirement and attrition.

WO:

### Issue

Health care.

If nothing is done about the cost of escalating health care, then no matter what else we do, this will sink us financially. We can bring home the troops, we can cap spending, we can reduce the size of government, but none of this will affect the outcome of BANKRUPTCY RUINATION if we don't deal with the Medicare/Medicaid and Social Security entitlement issues that must be made solvent. The stealing of real money from the Social Security Fund and replacing it with a piece of paper, an IOU, is testament to the lack of integrity that politicians are willing to go to in order to spend the people's money for furtherance of their own political careers.

### Possible solution

Put together a wise group of non-partisan people (no pusillanimous politicians) to study and make recommendations.

The goal is to:

A) Cover all Americans

1. For moral reasons
2. For economic reasons

The greater the pool of people, the easier to spread the risk. We are already paying for people with no insurance at the emergency room. How fair is it when a 22-year-old who has elected not to buy health insurance crashes his motorbike and we spend 100,000 to one million dollars trying to put his brains back in his skull? Everyone needs to pay something; there is no free lunch.

Make healthcare economically viable by cutting waste, fraud, bogus litigation, excessive profit, inefficiencies, and vast wasteful bureaucracies.

Free up the business sector from the responsibility of health care coverage. This will make American business more competitive globally. This will allow people to move.

If every American was covered with transportable health insurance, we would lift the lid on many would-be entrepreneurs who are eager to start a business but for being a healthcare hostage.

## Exercises to Strengthen the Heart (the Economy), the Muscle of Production.

E:

*Issue*

To stimulate or not to stimulate, that is the question?

*Possible solution*

There is no answer. Economists will argue for ever, and while they argue, nothing happens. The past is past so we must look to what to do in the future, preferably stimulating through incentives to entrepreneurs, without more debt.

WO:

*Issue*

The tax code is so massive, so convoluted, so complicated, that nobody understands it all, nobody. Therefore it is an act of violence against the people.

*Possible solution*

The best way to stimulate is to incentivize people to take economic action and risk. Given that we are in such huge debt, what I'm about to say may seem far fetched and is certainly counter-intuitive, but the best way to incentivize economic action and risk is to reduce taxes, not in the feeble normal way of a few percentage points here or the tweaking of the Social Security tax there (all designed to win political points); no, it must be dramatic and straightforward so that the message is clear: This is the New America and we are open for business.

Therefore, we suggest a flat rate income tax of 15% for everyone. This starts at the poverty level plus $12,000 for couples filing jointly and $6,000 for singles. The only deductions will be medical expenses, mortgage interest, insurance, and property taxes, Social Security and self employment taxes, state and local taxes, retirement contributions, and charitable donations.

E:

*Issue*

Jobs.

Jobs are created by entrepreneurs, not by government. Therefore, the opportunity must be there for those brave people to risk their money, time, and effort in starting a business. We need to stimulate the economy; therefore we need to stimulate the entrepreneurs.

Create an Entrepreneurs Fund of $50 Billion. If we can give billions and billions to failed companies like AIG, why can't we invest for job creation purposes? We have to remember that it's our money, not the government's.

Similarly, if we don't want established jobs and companies to go offshore, it must become more attractive for them to stay.

*Possible solution*

Fix the corporate tax rate at 15% with no excuses; every company has to pay.

WO: It is estimated that the government does not collect approximately one trillion dollars in taxes each year.

Why? Because there are so many loopholes available to corporations and wealthy individuals that they pay a fraction, if any, of what they owe. When companies and people don't pay their taxes it's usually for two reasons:

- They think the tax rate is too much
- There are legitimate loop holes to take advantage of for those with expert financial advisors.

This creates further unfairness with those that do pay.

E: I remember sitting down to lunch with some friends, one an avid Republican and the other equally as avid a Democrat. The subject of taxes came up and both said they did all they could to legitimately reduce their taxes. In fact, the Democrat stated that it had taken him quite a few years to finally figure out through his various companies a way to end up paying no tax at all.

When I asked if they would be happy to pay a flat rate of 15%, they both enthusiastically agreed that they would have no problem with that at all.

Therefore, we must make the dramatic change simple, less complex, and the opposite of an act of violence against the people: both effective and fair!

WO: This 15% income tax is the equivalent of putting a stent into the hearts blocked artery, suddenly allowing the free flow of oxygen (investment) to the body of the patient (the economy), a structural intervention that, if not done, will mean a slow, jobless recovery at best and a depression at worst.

If we can solve this most immediate problem of financial ruination, then we can move forward on evolving cooperative capitalism between nations for the solving of planetary environmental issues.

# APPENDIX A

# FURTHER POSSIBLE OUT-OF-THE-BOX IDEAS FOR HELPING THE ECONOMY

E:

*Issue*

The Federal Reserve is a privately-owned bank and we the public do not know who the owners are. This bank steps in and out of the market when it deems necessary, with no public oversight. In whose interest is it operating?

*Possible Solution*

The Federal Reserve Bank must belong to the people, not to some unknown private interest. And, the Federal Reserve must be run by a separate group, totally disconnected from the political process so that it does its job without political influence.

WO:

*Issue*

The housing market is part of the bedrock of the American economy. It is in disarray due to many factors, but it is necessary to stabilize it not just for economic factors, but also for social reasons. People need a place to live.

*Possible Solution*

Make a one-time, across-the-board mortgage rate offer of 3% to every homeowner in the country. If the government and Federal Reserve can make interest rate adjustments, why can't "We the People?" After all is said and done, it's our money.

Approximately 60% of all mortgages are held by Fannie and Freddie, which are owned by the Government, which means it's owned by "We the People."

Mortgages held in the private sector can do the same.

The difference between the 3% and existing mortgage rate can be repaid at the time of sale of the house or refinanced at any time between five and 30 years from implementation of the 3% mortgage. This gives everyone breathing room.

The economy is barely breathing and it will continue to just survive with minimal job growth for many years, maybe decades, unless we jumpstart it without creating more debt.

E:

*Issue*

Dependence on foreign oil.

*Possible Solution:*

Combine a weight-reduction measure with an exercise stimulus measure. Fix the price of gasoline at a constant $1 above the day-to-day market price. Take this extra dollar and split it: half to pay off the national debt and half for new renewable energy production that must be produced in this country. This will slow demand for oil; price is the best method for obtaining frugality, decreasing the threat to our national security from unstable oil regimes, increasing demand for more efficient alternative transportation, and showing that we are serious about paying down the national debt.

If people think this is too much to pay, make it 50 cents above the market price, but this little extra now will seem like nothing, absolutely nothing, in the face of default, loss of our reserve currency status, or hyperinflation, which can and will result if we don't take bold steps. This way everyone will know that each time they fill up their tank, they are helping the patient (the economy) get back on its feet.

WO:

*Issue*

Foreign aid. The real issue is not so much the foreign aid but the lack of results that the aid has achieved. Giving aid without education, particularly of women, without reversing land degradation, and without ensuring entrepreneurial sustainability merely creates unsustainable dependency.

*Possible Solution*

A cap on all foreign aid. Set up a special commission to look at all aid programs to ensure they meet the criteria:

- Education on the reversal of desertification.
- Education, with special emphasis on educating and empowering women, which has been shown to reduce family size.
- Education on entrepreneurialism together with microlending.

E:

*Issue*

Private capital needed to help pay the national debt.

*Possible Solution*

During World War II we had War Bonds. Let us institute a Peace Bond. All legal residents of the United States can buy up to one million dollars per individual, and the same for corporations. This money is for the sole purpose of paying down our foreign national debt. Instead of being owned by foreign governments, a national security issue, we will be owned by Americans. We will be showing the world that we are serious about paying off our debt, which will boost confidence in the long term viability of America and the global financial system.

If 100 million people/corporations invested $10,000 each, that would bring in one trillion dollars. This special bond would pay 2% above the prime rate and would be non-taxable.

Even if the foreign debt is owed at a lower rate than the Peace Bond rate, at least it is paying off the foreign creditor while paying interest to the people of America who will put that money to work. Don't listen to the howls from Wall Street. It's our country, our government, and our money.

# APPENDIX B

# FURTHER IDEAS FOR CONSIDERATION REGARDING POLITICIANS

WO:

*Issue*

Everyone knows that without money, you can't get elected. Therefore, those who contribute the most have bigger hold over that candidate than the ordinary person with his or her one vote in the crowd.

Democracy becomes a sham when big money rules the day. Unless we make structural changes, versus superficial platonic platitudes, we are doomed.

*Possible Solution*

Therefore, we need publicly funded elections so that there is a level playing ground for all candidates, with no influence peddling.

Members of the public can give up to a suitable amount, say $100, in donations to their particular candidate.

E:

*Issue*

Elected politicians still need money for re-election (under the current system) and are therefore beholden to lobbyist who give them money for the lobbyist's pet cause.

This further dilutes the ordinary citizen's voice, as the money comes from special interests, e.g., Wall Street, big banks, the auto industry, the health care industry, and the insurance industry.

*Possible Solution*

Not allowing lobbyist to lobby could be seen as an impediment to freedom of speech. Therefore, a special large room is set aside for lobbyists and elected officials to meet to discuss the proposals put forth by the lobbyist in full public view, recorded on C-Span for total transparency.

No elected official is allowed to take any money whatsoever from anyone, other than the allowed amount from private citizens' campaign contributions.

WO:

*Issue*

Politicians gain favor with their constituents by bringing home the bacon. This leads to unmitigated adding on of earmarks, inserts, and amendments onto bills that have nothing to do with the original bill.

*Possible Solution*

Nothing can be added that is not absolutely germane to the bill in question.

E:

*Issue*

Incumbents. They have failed; there are no excuses.

*Answer*

Vote out the incumbents in both parties, no exceptions, to send a message that we are serious about taking back power from the politicians, special interests, and money influencers. Vote in the new breed of politicians from both parties who vow to fulfill the manifesto, the will of the people, who will be known as "For the Country Politicians."

### Wrap Up

E:  What happens if we don't pay heed and we continue down the profligate path?

WO:  No one knows when the shifting sands of the financial foundation will wash away. No one knows what financial lunacy will trip the wire or burst the dam. One only knows that all illusions shatter and painful lessons are learned.

> Just as war teaches there are no winners,
> Only the shattered, wounded and dead,
> No land obtained, no people conquered,
> 'Cept groans of those on whom we tread.
>
> When all the Universe relies on balance
> To keep its steady path,
> What possible other outcome can there be,
> But reckoning of the math.
>
> When the lords of money create phantom wealth
> And greed becomes their god,
> All manner of imbalance thus applies,
> The stricken ledger we plod.

Imagine a global tsunami wave
Traveling the financial seas,
Its size and shape foreboding,
The bringing to our knees.

We have seen the wave in motion,
Gathering height and speed,
But all waves crest,
And rage the rocks indeed.

This visionary wave portrays,
The mountainous debt therein,
Held up by pure momentum,
Its substance merely skin.

By diligent honest work and thoughtful action now, we can repay our debts and change the future. It's up to us.

All outstanding debts must be wiped from the slate, until the ocean is calm and gentle once more.

Quote from: **The Message of the Divine Iliad, by Walter Russell.**

*THE LAW OF BALANCE is the Law of Love upon which the Universe is founded. This law is given to man for his coming renaissance of greater comprehension. It is of all laws, the most inclusive, and the most simple. It consists of but three words. These three words are the very foundation of all our material existence, all phenomena of matter or interchange between humans, economically, socially and spiritually.*

The three words are:

RHYTHMIC BALANCED INTERCHANGE

www.ingramcontent.com/pod-product-compliance
Lightning Source LLC
LaVergne TN
LVHW020936090426
835512LV00020B/3378